Finding the
Water

D1714892

Rev. Mark Stang, BCC
as told to Carol Sanders

ISBN 978-1-64559-703-2 (Paperback)
ISBN 978-1-64559-704-9 (Digital)

Covenant Books, Inc.
11661 Hwy 707
Murrells Inlet, SC 29576
www.covenantbooks.com

To all those who have and are praying for me. That could be you who are reading these words. Sometimes I wonder, does praying for someone really work? People say, "I'll pray for you," and they talk to God, "Lord, please bless this person," or "Bless my children." Does that simple task really change things? I think of those people who physically are no longer able to do what they used to do, and of women and men in their golden years. When they shift their mission in life to pray for others, what a blessing that is to the world. I think of the funerals of people who had a deep prayer life. As we send them off to their reward, I am so grateful to them, and I wonder who will take their place. Anyone who has prayed for me, may God bless you in return a hundredfold.

Also to my little sister Jean (Stang) Malone + who was thirty-eight and pregnant with her second child when she was diagnosed with glioblastoma brain cancer. Jean was my support, my rock. Oftentimes she knew when I was overstressed. She would say to me, "Mark, 'Puah,' just let it go." Jean certainly had a vision and a clear mission in her life. She would always reach out to the less fortunate and the poor. Wherever she went, she left a trail of the inspiration and goodness behind her. Jean died on March 19, 2004.

Acknowledgment

While on sabbatical in 2010, Father Mark wrote down his life story, which was then recorded by Sr. Anne Murtagh. Her initial write-up was immensely helpful in the preparation of this book. May God rest her beautiful soul.

INTRODUCTION

As a hospital chaplain, I feel honored to be invited to be present for patients and their families in such an important time of their lives. Each of the patients with terminal illness handles it in a different way.

In December 2018, I was invited to the room of "Peter," who had rare blood cancer. As I was visiting with him and his wife, he spoke strongly, "I can't die. I have so much more to live for. I enjoy cutting lawns, and I have a goal to continue to cut my lawn and the lawns of my neighbors." I encouraged Peter to keep that desire in his heart and to stay positive, for that would help not only his spirit but also his body.

A few weeks later, Peter was admitted to the hospital again. He requested that I visit him. He had a very difficult time breathing. He said, "I don't want to give up."

"Peter, think about not giving up but giving over. Give everything over to God, putting everything in God's hands."

Just a few days after my previous visit, Peter invited me back into his room. His wife and children were around his bed. As I approached, Peter reached out to me and grasped both my hands. He spoke with labored breath.

"Is it time to stop?"

I asked him what he meant by that, and he just repeated, "Is it time to stop?"

"Peter, you will never stop. You will live on and on and on. Your body will stop, but you—your spirit, your soul—will never stop. You will step into the next world. Let go…and give yourself over to God."

The next day, I was walking down the hall on my way to another patient. The nurse stopped me and said, "Oh, I'm glad you are here—we need you." She brought me into Peter's room. I laid my hands upon his head, and I spoke into his ear, "Into your hands, Lord, I commend my spirit." Peter's breathing was very shallow—one breath every fifteen seconds. As we were praying the Litany of Saints, Peter's eyelids were closed, but I could see that his eyes were moving rapidly back and forth. Then his heart stopped, and his face relaxed.

Peter's wife said, "Father, thank you so much for being here. You gave me and Peter so much comfort."

I always feel so honored to be present when someone dies. I think, what did Peter see? I become inspired when I hear or read about a near-death experience.

Being invited into many different lives and their backgrounds, I have learned that everybody has a story, and I'm fascinated by listening to people's history and how they were formed. I write this book with several people who requested and encouraged me to put my own story—or as I really like to say, "God's story"—into book form.

Boy on the Farm

My journey to the priesthood is unusual, but when we look back to the very beginning, it might seem almost planned. The beginning, of course, is my conception, for all life begins at conception.

I was conceived in a seminary.

Now let me explain. My mom and dad showed us children what a beautiful marriage can be like. I'm sure they had their disagreements, but they never argued in front of us children. They enjoyed similar things together like visiting with family and friends, playing cards, and especially music. They truly enjoyed dancing. Their love for each other was very evident and expressed in many ways.

Another way their love was expressed was in September of 1957. My mom and dad traveled with my aunts and uncles to Hastings, Nebraska, to visit my dad's brother, Br. Dan, OSC. Mom and Dad spent the weekend at the seminary in some rooms that had been converted into guest quarters. Nine months later, on June 2, 1958, Andrew and Edith (Winkelman) Stang were proud parents of their fifth child, Mark James Stang.

The family grew to ten children—six girls and four boys: Karen, Steve, Marlene, Mike, Mark, Jeff, Lori, Jeanie, Stacie, and Sandra (who is now called Sister Perpetua O.P.).

In my early formative years—until I was six years old—I grew up in a safe place that some people may even call a bubble. Our family social life consisted of close neighbors, church members, and cousins, some of whom were also our neighbors. At the time, I didn't realize how protected I was.

We grew up on a farm near St. Nicholas, a town of about a hundred people in Stearns County, in central Minnesota. Our farm had it all: 160 acres, thirty-two dairy cows, chickens, pigs, two horses, one dog, and a bunch of other pets over the years. I loved to be outside, playing "farmer in the ground." I took my little red tractor and plow down to the granary where the sand was soft from the road runoff after a hard rain.

I also recall lying on the grass, looking up to the clouds, and wondering what heaven is like. The clouds were cumulus puffy ones that you can discover animals in. To this very day, clouds fascinate me—how they can change forms in minutes, how the sunlight glistens and reflects back from them. The bigger the thunderhead, the more glorious.

Looking up at the clouds when I was young, I would ask myself if there is a heaven and what it's going to be like there. Angels playing harps? I would get a warm feeling in my heart—until my back got cold and wet. Looking up, I would ask myself, *Is Joanne there?* My aunt Joanne died very young, leaving two young sons behind. I went to her wake. I didn't see her body in that box because I was too short, but I remember looking around and feeling the sadness in the room.

Later I would ponder and actually want to talk to Joanne: "Where are you?" I felt a deep connection to the beyond. The idea of heaven made me feel a closeness, like a friendship. A safe place. To this day I enjoy contemplating the sky.

Growing up in the country, I spent most of my time outdoors. We had a daily routine of chores, taking care of the animals, and playing with the pets. Pepper, our black Lab, would enjoy playing "figure 8." He would race in a circle pattern on our big lawn and get just close enough to us that we could almost touch him. If we dived toward him when he got close, we could possibly touch his back leg. This was our simple country life.

My father always encouraged us kids to join in with the work, but we never lacked time for play. He would give us time to play softball in the spring and summer and football in the fall. With nine brothers and sisters, I never had a hard time finding others to play with. At night after chores, we would at times cross the field to our neighbors' place, or they would come to our place. They were also our cousins—ten children in their family too. I really enjoyed playing these games. I wasn't the best athlete, but we had a great time.

Farm life meant chores. Dad was not one to buy new machinery; he liked to go to farm auctions. He would get a good deal on used machinery to keep us boys busy learning how to repair it. Instead of telling us what to do, he would be patient and show us how. Once he knew we could handle the responsibility safely, he allowed us to do the work. Dad was generous with praise—and fifty cents a week. Each lesson made us feel a little more grown up.

I felt like an adult the first time that I got to drive a tractor. We were picking rocks in an open field—that's also how my older siblings learned to drive. I was eight years old and barely able to reach the clutch and the brake of the H Farmall tractor. At first, I thought it was more fun imagining driving a tractor when I played with my toys. Now I was responsible for my safety and the safety of the equipment, but most especially the safety of others. This made me nervous. Later on that evening, Dad told Mom at the supper table that I had done a good job. I felt proud that Dad trusted me. My other siblings smiled and then teased me, "He drove so crooked we thought he was on the road to Richmond." This positive experience gives me a sense of accomplishment even today as I enjoy being out in the field on my day off, driving a tractor.

My mother was a kindhearted woman who never played favorites. She treated all of us children the same. We knew we could go to her with any problem. She was wise enough to know when we were just whining about something; she would often remind us, "Don't make a mountain out of a molehill." I find myself in situations today where this wisdom helps me to stay calm and focused.

Mom was a wonderful cook. Freshly baked bread was a treat. We could add butter that would melt on the soft, warm bread and create a snack of buttery goodness that welcomed us home from school. Her specialty was pies—real lemon, apple, and rhubarb with raisins. Mom truly made our house a home, even when money got a little tight and she had to take a job off the farm. She worked in Eden Valley at Animal Fair, where they manufactured stuffed animals. She liked the job because Dad said she could do with the money whatever she wanted. Soon we had new pots and pans and dishes.

I never saw myself as a spiritual person or having grown up in a spiritual family. I saw ours as a normal family. We were not perfect. We had our arguments. As a young boy, I remember praying the rosary every day, especially during Lent. We would usually say this prayer after supper. Dad would lead, and all of us would kneel down around the table with our elbows on our chairs. I was one of the biggest complainers. This was much more of a pain for me than a spiritual experience. I would much rather be outside working. Some evenings we would forget, or we would have to start the chores because we were running late. Dad would remember to pray the rosary that evening before we went to bed. I did not see the fruit of this prayer at the time. I remember one time asking God, "If I say this rosary, could you give me an A on my test?" It never happened. I struggled with my faith at times. Why didn't God answer my prayers in the way I wanted them to be answered?

I was the quiet one of the family. I felt comfortable interacting with my family at home, but I wouldn't say much. One time during a meal at the kitchen table, my older brother asked me, "Mark, why don't you say something?" I replied, "I don't get a chance—you guys talk too fast!" I had to ponder my thoughts before I spoke them. When we went to visit people, speaking up was even more difficult. It took me a while to warm up to strangers. My brother Mike was more outgoing. I enjoyed hanging around Mike as I let him do all the talking. I am not sure why I was so shy. When I would get the courage to speak, I would talk with my eyes focused on the ground more than on the person!

School...ugh. My first-grade classroom was a crowded one-room schoolhouse with one teacher for eight grades. Then for both second and third grades, I had a teacher that wasn't at all like Mom. In fact, she scared me. "Mrs. Dornfeld" was a large woman, and I don't remember ever seeing her smile. She intimidated me. She was to the point of being abusive, sometimes calling the class a bunch of calves.

Much of my dislike of school was my fault. I didn't give school my full attention and effort. One beautiful spring day, I was staring out the window at the clouds. Mrs. Dornfeld called on me with a question that was written on the board. I was not able to answer. I gave it my best shot and must have said something stupid, and the rest of the class laughed at me. I was coming to realize that I was not on the same level as my classmates. This gave me all the more reason not to say anything. The teacher must have had a discussion with my mother, for soon after, I got my eyes checked and so did my younger brother Jeff. We both went to the optometrist and came home with glasses. This didn't help my self-image. They were heavy and kept sliding down my nose when I ran.

In the summer between second and third grade, the school-house burned. We began the next school year using the church basement. One spring day, I noticed smoke near the ceiling. I called this to the teacher's attention, but I was ignored. I felt rejected yet still concerned. Less than a minute later, we heard shouts of "Fire!" from the next room. We students grabbed our coats and ran across the parking lot. We watched as all the area fire departments fought the blaze.

Thank God the firemen were able to save the church. However, the inside of the church had to be completely redone. It was decided that our little school district would be no more. We would need to split up. My classmates went in three different directions. Most of them were sent to Cold Spring which was seven miles away. Some went to Eden Valley which was six miles in a different direction. Just a few of us went to school fifteen miles away in Kimball, Minnesota. I dreaded being separated from my friends.

As I began fourth grade in Kimball, I encountered a very wonderful, understanding teacher. "Mrs. Rangler" was so very patient with me. I was reading at only a first-grade level. This was embarrassing and made school much harder, but Mrs. Rangler helped me improve my reading. Part of me felt embarrassed because I had to be sent out of the room for tutoring, but another part of me was becoming enlightened because now I knew what people meant when they talked about Dick and Jane.

As I grew, I was quite thin. I could eat but not gain weight. Kids in school called me "the Runt." One person said I had worms. This degrading treatment led me to believe that I was somehow different from—and inferior to—other kids. The name that hurt the most was "stupid." It made me feel small and incapable. I came to believe those ugly words.

In fifth grade I had an opportunity to learn an instrument for the band. Mom encouraged this for us kids. My older brother Mike played the drums, and I was impressed how my sister Marlene could play the clarinet. I chose the cornet because it had only three buttons; I figured that would be the easiest instrument to play. Unable to read notes, I struggled to correlate what was on the page to which button to push. Maryann, the girl I sat beside in band, was a very good trumpet player. I decided that instead of looking at the notes on the paper, I would just watch her to see which finger to put down. It was difficult to keep up with her. It didn't take long before the band director asked me to stay after class. He invited me into his office, where he told me that I had a beautiful voice and I should join the choir instead.

Bus rides were the worst. A boy named "Rollie," who was a year ahead of me, was not mean when my older brothers were riding with us, but when they were dropped off at the high school, Rollie would call me "stupid" and "no good" (and other words I don't feel comfortable putting down on paper) and swear at me. He would punch me at times, but I could not swing back because I could not match his strength. He left me feeling worthless. Why did I believe this boy's epithets?

One day in fifth grade, as school was getting out, the buses had picked us grade school students up. For some reason, they were not able to park where they usually picked up the high school students. The bus had to park and wait on a downward slope. While waiting, our driver got out to chat with the other drivers. The bus began to roll downhill toward another bus. It started out very slowly, but as we progressed down, the bus started picking up speed. Students began

14

screaming, running forward and jumping out the open front door. As I ran toward the front of the bus, I found myself jumping over the shift lever and landing into the empty driver's seat. I put my foot on the brake pedal and pushed as hard as I could. Thanks to God for the training I had received on the farm.

The bus stopped inches before it rammed another bus. We were all stunned at what had almost happened. I thought to myself, *Wow—did I just do that?* I felt so proud to have prevented an accident. I kept my foot on the brake as the other kids started getting back on the bus.

Rollie stomped onto the bus and frowned at me. "Aw, s——t. Stupid runt! Why the h—l didn'tcha let the bus crash?"

This was not at all the response I had expected. Neither was the punch in the arm Rollie gave me as he passed the driver's seat. Even when I did something good, someone found a way to stomp on me. But I didn't let that get me down. I felt so proud of myself. As I stayed sitting on the edge of that seat with my right foot fully extended and my hands on that huge steering wheel, I was thinking that the bus driver might say to me—just as Dad would say—"Great job, Mark, thanks so much."

The bus driver got on. Now I would be praised for taking action. But instead of seeing the face of gratitude, I saw a face that was red, embarrassed, and angry. The driver shook his finger in my face. "What're you doin' in my seat? Did you take off the hand brake and make it roll? You think you can drive, huh? Get outta there! You oughta know better."

The driver must have been embarrassed about the mishap and needed to blame someone for his own negligence.

Lord, thank you for the healing that came with my forgiving the boy and the driver. They did not know what they were doing. I still know I did the right thing.

15

Not Enough

As junior high progressed, I was a below-average student. I was pleased to know when I could pass to the next grade. Still, reading intimidated me. Whenever I would read, it was very difficult to make sense of the words and comprehend them in my head. This made my mind wander. I was putting a lot of pressure on myself and believed that I was dumb. Books and I were just not friends.

I was much more comfortable at home, helping Dad on the farm. Most of all I enjoyed working with the soil. We were blessed to farm good, rich, loamy/clay soil. At times I would get off the tractor to walk around and just smell the freshly plowed field. It smelled sweet—"the smell of life." I would closely examine a handful of soil and see all the living organisms, including the worms, and also knew there were many other organisms that I didn't see. I was holding a ball of life. My dad taught me to respect soil. He was very careful to protect the soil from erosion and to keep the nutrients in it balanced and healthy. Maybe that's why I always felt connected to the soil.

There's nothing like getting up early in the morning and smelling the fresh, crisp air. The only sound you hear is the cattle letting you know that they are happy that you're coming to feed them and bring them contentment. That same contentment came upon me after a hard day's work, knowing that I made a positive impact. On the farm, unlike at school, I made a positive difference.

Physically, I was not as strong or as fast as my friends. I did not really develop until well into eleventh grade. In seventh grade, I realized I lacked the coordination for basketball, so I wrestled, but only because my brothers did. It was just something Stang men did. This Stang man did not bring home any medals, though. I chose wrestling only because it was a winter sport. In the spring and in the fall, I wanted to work in the fields.

Just after my sixteenth birthday. I tried out for the St. Nicholas baseball team which played every Sunday afternoon. This was the highlight of the community social gathering. The team, called the "Nicks," consisted of the Schreiners, the Theisess, the Schwartzes, and also the Stangs, my older brothers. I stepped up to the plate when it was my turn for the tryouts. "Henry" was the one pitching to me. As a fan from boyhood, I had never seen Henry on the mound. I was expecting generous pitches to hit. Instead, Henry threw me hard, fast junk. I didn't come close. After a few minutes, the manager said, "Mark, stick with softball."

I left, very dejected at my failure and very angry with Henry. Another place I didn't belong.

Future Farmers of America (FFA) was where this Stang man belonged. One thing scared me, though: all students had to memorize the FFA pledge before they could join. The pledge was only about thirty words, and my friends learned it easily. I studied many anxious nights after chores at the kitchen table trying to memorize the pledge. I *so* wanted to be accepted into this farming group. I honestly don't know how I did it, but when I was asked I recited the pledge—not perfectly, but enough to get in. Here is where I truly belonged and felt at home.

Girls…because of my shyness, this was another challenge for me. I had a crush on a few girls but was much too shy to talk to them. I stayed home from both the junior and senior prom—not only because of being shy, but I also thought if I asked one girl out, then the others would feel bad. And I didn't want anybody to feel bad. I always felt a lot more comfortable when my friends would have gatherings as a group.

In my senior year, to my surprise, I was voted FHA (Future Homemakers of America) Sweetheart. We FFA boys had voted a sweetheart girl, and it happened to be someone I had a crush on—"Jennifer," who had long brown hair, a beautiful smile with dimples, and a wholesome beauty about her.

After we "sweetheart" winners were announced, there was an FHA and FFA Sweetheart Dance. The tradition during this gathering was that the sweethearts would have the first dance. When the music began, my friends said, "Mark, get out there and dance." This dance song was not a polka that my sisters taught me how to dance; no, this was a slow dance. The song they played was called "If" by one of my favorite bands, Bread. As I walked out, I met Jennifer in the middle of the floor. I was so nervous. I had butterflies in my stomach, and I could feel myself sweating.

We were the only ones on the floor. I was overwhelmed not only about dancing but about being the center of attention. I remember my older sisters told me when you dance, just go with the beat, so I let my body flow with the beat. Jennifer seemed to enjoy it. She thanked me with a smile. After the song finished and as I was coming off the floor, my friends cheered and said, "Good job, Mark." I felt peace and great joy in my heart. I also felt humbled to think that I was chosen for this honor. To have my friends who were not jealous but supportive of me made me feel appreciated and part of the group. It was a very special night for me.

What would I do with myself after high school? I very much wanted to take over the farm, but my older brother Mike was already preparing to do that. College was definitely out of the question; book learning was not for me. I had learned some carpentry. I could do that like many of my friends, but I really loved the land. So what to do? I asked my high school agriculture teacher, and he encouraged me to go to agronomy school. He recommended a vo-tech school in Canby, a town about three hours away. This school offered an eleven-month soil science agronomy program. I thought, *That's less than a year—I can do that.*

After graduation from high school, a friend at a party told me that "Sharon" had a crush on me and wanted to go out with me. I was a bit surprised. Me? Wow. What should I do? Should I ask her out? Would she really say yes to me? She lived and went to school in Cold Spring, so I really didn't know her very well.

Sharon was a beautiful, sweet, blond and blue-eyed girl with a quick smile. I thought she was possibly the high school beauty queen in her school. It took me about two months to get up the nerve to act. Finally, as I was just about to leave for tech school, and with the encouragement of my friends, I realized I had better ask her out. I called Sharon, and she accepted the date.

I was ready to take her out to a movie in St. Cloud. I had my red 1969 Chevy Malibu all cleaned up and looking sharp. I was more nervous than excited. I put on my favorite shirt and jeans. When I stopped at her house to pick her up, I was so nervous I almost turned around and left. I took a deep breath, walked up to her sidewalk, and rang the doorbell.

Sharon opened the door with a smile and invited me in, which I didn't expect. She led me downstairs where I thought, *Oh shoot, I have to meet her mom and dad.* I took a deep breath and said to myself, *Here I go.* The staircase and basement were somewhat dark. As I landed on the bottom step, the lights went on. A room full of her friends and mine hollered, "Surprise!"

Sharon and her friends had planned a going-away party for me, and what a surprise it was.

I was shocked and breathless. I had a hard time saying any words to anyone. They all had a great time surprising me. I felt so loved and supported. It was overwhelming. I could not believe that these people showed so much love to me. We played games with music and danced into the night and did a lot of laughing.

At the end of the night, as we were leaving, her friends urged me to ask Sharon out on a "real" date for the following night. I just couldn't bring myself through all that nervousness again.

Mark, if you only knew then what you know now: simply to trust in God and everything is going to be okay.
Trust in me.

3

"The Best You Can Be"

I regretted not having the courage to ask Sharon out again. Off I went to Canby Vo Tech. However, during my first week at school, I called her, and we corresponded by letter. On the weekends I came home, we dated.

My soil science instructor was from India. He wore a turban. I took great interest in him. Students would make fun of him, but I didn't hold any bias and thought he was a very intelligent man, though he lacked American common sense. He knew science and especially soil science, but he struggled with practical things like adjusting a desk. One day I had to help him open a container. He also asked me to help him start his car, which simply had a loose cable. We became good friends.

I felt honored to be friends with someone so different. I had so many questions about his culture, and he was so very interesting. I have found this to be true many times in my life with people of different cultures.

This professor worked a lot with developing new hybrid seeds and needed help in the greenhouse on campus. I volunteered and enjoyed working in the greenhouse—I loved the smell of the soil. It was a bit of heaven to be able to play with the soil in the middle of the winter. Helping the instructor also didn't hurt me in my goal to achieve a passing grade.

Another of the courses I took at the end of agronomy school was Sales and Communications. We learned communication skills and how to work with the farmers to sell the product. The instructor was a highly motivational man who encouraged us to believe in ourselves. He said, "If you don't believe in yourself, how are you to expect other people to believe in you? You need to be the best you can be—it's up to you."

This course gave me a different perspective of myself. I said to myself, "I'm really not sure I can do this, but I'm going to give it my best." My shyness and self-doubt were beginning to wane. I came to realize more and more that I don't do well with books, but I learn best with hands-on experience.

As I approached graduation from vo-tech, I was informed of a fertilizer and feed plant manager position. I drove out to Augusta, Wisconsin, for a job interview. Wisconsin is a beautiful state to drive through. As I drove into town, I noticed many mom-and-pop places as I drove up to the plant. I was greeted by a friendly receptionist and asked to sit down. The stomach started to ache, and my breathing was short, but I kept telling myself, "Mark, just breathe."

When I walked into the interview room, I saw five men, mostly elderly, looking very serious. All five were sitting on one side of a large table. On my side was one chair which I presumed was for me. I sat down, feeling very nervous and intimidated. I answered their questions the best I could. I heard myself telling the board of directors that I knew I could handle the job. I was amazed to hear such words coming from shy, quiet Mark. One member said as I walked out of the room, "I like you, but you are very young for this position. Why don't you wait in the next room." As I sat in the office, I watched an older, more professional man walk in and be escorted to the conference room to interview. I was sure he would get the position.

After an hour, they called me back into the room and offered me the job! Here I was at nineteen years old, managing a plant. I was honored, yet I thought, *Mark, what have you gotten yourself into?*

I started work in the fall. I got my feet on the ground overseeing only two full-time employees. One had been working there for thirty-three years and was ready to retire, and the other was a severe alcoholic. To be honest, I didn't feel very welcome. I can understand how they may have felt: "Who is this young whippersnapper telling us what to do?" The number of employees increased as the planting season began.

I decided to use the skills my dad taught me. I chose not to tell them what to do but to work with them. I soon learned the most difficult cleaning task and the most difficult parts of the job.

One service this plant provided for farmers was to bring a large truck to their farmyard and load it up with their cob corn, bring it back to the plant, grind it, mix it with the ration for the farmer's cows, and then deliver it back to the farm.

No one wanted to go to a farm owned by "Lawrence." The farmer would have his cob corn not in a crib with a floor but lying on the ground. One cold February morning, the call came in from Lawrence's Dairy. I decided to take on this task myself rather than sending someone else out to the farm. Shoveling snow-covered corn was not an easy task. The cobs were frozen into the ground. The job took me several hours; my fingers became cold and then numb. When I got back to the plant, one of the guys said, "So, Mark, how are you doing?" I didn't swear as I had heard others do. I just smiled back and said, "Yep, I know what you guys have to go through. We're going to have to make some changes here. But I got the load full, and we will still give the best service possible."

I could sense the change of attitude and the increased respect the guys had for me. From that day on, when I asked employees to do something, instead of shaking their heads and grumbling, they would more readily say yes. I felt good about initiating this change. Could it be true that you have to earn your respect?

I lived in a low-income housing apartment that at one time had been a hotel. I had a room just big enough to hold a bed and a sink. I shared a bathroom with other boarders down the hall. Just inside the front door was a reception area which included a sitting room with a television. For food I would go down to the local café, or to the grocery store and buy bread, peanut butter, and other things that I could keep up in my room. I wanted to save as much money as possible, and this was the best rate in town. I was a bit embarrassed by this meager life, and I did miss Mom's cooking, but I took it in stride and knew I was saving money.

One night, Derek, a friend who lived down the hall, invited me to a party. I found out soon that this wasn't like a party back home. We went to a house, and before long we were invited to come to the living room and sit around in a circle. I could smell some smoke odor that I had never smelled before. The guys passed a funny-looking pipe around the circle. Again I found myself thinking, *Mark, what have you gotten yourself into?*

Fear of the consequences—physical, legal, and social—of an illicit drug had me very concerned. When the pipe came to me, I took it and quietly said, "No, thanks," and passed it on to the next guy. Thankfully I was not pressured or teased for my refusal.

I had to help Derek home that night. His speech was slurred. He was weak and vomiting. I was relieved when I finally got him into his bed. When I checked on him in the morning, he still was sick and asked me what happened. He was seriously ill. I kept checking in on him. When I told him I thought I was going to have to bring him to the doctor, he said, "No, no, no, please don't!" So I became his nurse and got him what he needed for three days. I was so glad I had turned down the marijuana or whatever other drugs were at that party. I remain afraid of marijuana or any other drug. When I went to parties, I did enjoy beer, and that was enough. As I work with people now, I realize how easy it is to be innocent and curious but how quickly a little experimentation can lead to a serious illness or addiction.

After a year and a half working in Wisconsin, I received a phone call from the chairperson of the board of directors of the fertilizer plant in Cold Spring, Minnesota. He offered me a job managing the plant, which is just seven miles from my home farm. At first I felt overwhelmed, but later I felt excited to be able to move back closer to the farm. This also gave me a chance to build my relationship with Sharon, as this was her hometown. This new job also offered me quite a bit more in salary.

At the Cold Spring co-op, I was making good money. Managing the plant was challenging, working with staff and our clients and trying to please them. It was at times very draining for me. During the planting season, the work was intense with long hours trying to please all the farmers who wanted their product ASAP. The days were long. One week I clocked over 120 hours.

After a year and a half in the plant manager position, I learned that my brother Mike had decided not to continue farming. Dad asked if I would be willing to go into partnership with him and take over our home farm. This was my dream come true. I wanted to farm with Dad and raise a family like the one I grew up in.

I decided to invest in the farm. It was a financial risk, as the interest rate to borrow money was over 10 percent. I wondered what the market was going to do. Despite all the risk, I felt good about the decision. This would put me back in the field more than in a truck or behind a desk.

One cold March evening, I decided to go out to the hog barn and check on one of the sows. My hunch was correct: the sow was starting to give birth. I put a heat lamp above the sow as she lay on the golden straw. Then I took each piglet and wiped it clean and set it up to the sow's belly to nurse. This particular sow surprised me as I helped her deliver 13 piglets. The last one was a runt. Knowing the struggles of being a runt, I gave that one a little more tender loving care.

I continued dating Sharon, and she was supportive and open for invites to the farm.

I put a lot of my energy into the farm. I remembered what my vo-tech teacher had said: "Be the best you can be." I was going to be the best farmer I could be.

Lord, I am finally finding some meaning and some direction in my life. Help me to be the best I can be.

The "Tug"

I continued dating Sharon, and all things were fine. My dream was coming true. I played softball in the evenings with my friends and sometimes in the weekend tournaments if I could fit it in between chores. I would also enjoy my dirt bike, riding around on a Sunday afternoon with some friends. I had many friends with different interests. I had it made, being a successful farmer and everything else one could ask for.

And yet…there was something deep within me that wasn't content—a deep yearning that was so quietly tugging, calling me to do more for others, more for the world. I ignored it, quickly filling my days up with all that had to get done.

To help pay for the seed corn for the spring, I sold my '69 Chevelle. I would go to softball games and out on dates with the farm truck. It was a nice-looking pickup with green and white trim and lots of chrome. However, if I would haul hogs during the day, no matter how hard I cleaned it, it was not a sweet-smelling vehicle at night.

I felt sorry for Sharon, not only because of the smelly truck but because I was not giving her the attention she deserved. Part of me was thinking, *Mark, this is the right thing to do—get married and have a family. Raise our children on the farm, just like Mom and Dad.* And yet every time I would go into quiet to let go of life's distractions,

I felt a pull toward something more. I did not know yet what that something was.

Should I ask Sharon to marry me? I felt I had to make a decision. We had been dating for two years. Still, I could not get engaged when I did not feel 100 percent committed and at peace with the decision. I had not told Sharon about the tug. She didn't say it, but I believed she knew I was struggling.

One evening on a date, I told Sharon I needed time and that I needed to give her freedom. I felt this was not fair to her to string her along as I tried to make up my mind. One softball teammate in particular was pressuring me to make a decision. I tried to be as honest as possible and at the same time as kind as possible. I told her I needed time.

About a week later, on a hot August day, Dad and I were out in the field working on a tile line in a six-foot-deep trench. It was a wet, muddy job, as the clay soil stuck to everything. It was about noon, and we were ready to take a lunch break. As I got up out of the trench, I noticed Sharon's car coming up the driveway. I was curious because I had thought we were not going to see each other for a while. So I set down my shovel and tried to scrape the dirt off my hands. When I came into the yard, Dad went into the house to wash up.

Sharon was waiting by her car in the yard. She looked serious and sad. I felt a bit embarrassed; my sleeveless shirt was soaked with sweat, and my hands were grimy.

I said, "Hi."

"Goodbye, Mark."

I could not get any words out of my mouth. We endured a long, long silence.

When I looked at her, I could see her pain. That hurt me deeply because I was the one that had caused her pain.

Sharon handed me the gifts that I had given her over the last two years. Her soft, white hands placed a necklace and earrings into my calloused, muddy hands.

I tried to use a clean part of my forearms to wipe the tears from my eyes. All I said was, "Sharon, I'm sorry." She got into her car and drove away.

I felt heavyhearted and sad. I had hurt her. I wondered what I could do or say to help her feel better.

I did not eat very much for lunch that day or anything that night. I was sad that I had broken someone's heart. I wasn't proud of many things I had done in my life, and this was one of them.

Months later, I felt ready to date other girls. I would initiate the date because they showed interest in me, which only lead to more broken hearts—caused by me. I was just trying to ignore the "something more" feeling.

One afternoon at a church gathering, a farmer tried to connect me with his daughter, who he said would be a good farmer's wife. I felt honored because he was known as one of the best farmers in the area, and that's what I wanted to be. Still, I did not ask her out. I needed to be more at peace with myself and who I am as a person before I could get involved in another relationship. I also did not want to hurt anyone again.

When I would allow myself to be very quiet and honest with myself, I noticed something deeper happening—something that I couldn't put into words...something spiritual.

A very slight "tug" on my heart.

I—Mark—the boy who complained about the rosary and wondered why God didn't answer prayers the way I wanted—felt something spiritual.

I did have relatives on both my dad's and my mom's side of the family who were living the religious life. When they would come and visit, they always seemed happy. But religious life had never even crossed my mind as a vocation for me. My brother Mike was the one in our family that we thought might become a priest. Mike is a great people person and funny.

My younger sister Jean was my close companion on the farm. She was more comfortable working outside with me doing chores rather than inside the house. We had many good close talks about many things: her friends, the softball team, and the basketball team.

After she graduated from high school, she became a college athlete. She was not afraid of work, and she lived life to the fullest. We used to listen to Jay Kesler, a spiritual psychologist, on the radio in the barn. Every evening at the same time, his radio program would have listeners call in and describe personal problems, and then there was a one-minute advertisement. During the ad, Jean and I would share how we would solve the problem and then listen to Jay's response. I think many times we had a better answer. For example, one lady called in and said her daughter was getting married in a few months. The caller had recently learned that she had breast cancer and had to have surgery. She wanted to postpone the treatment and not tell her daughter—this way her daughter wouldn't have to worry and could focus on the wedding. Jean and I both agreed to advise the caller to let her daughter know as soon as possible. The next minute, we found out we were right—Jay's response was similar to ours. Hm... maybe I *was* spiritual.

The tug continued despite my attempts to ignore it. One beautiful June evening after milking the cows, I was cultivating corn on the bottom forty. Cultivating corn requires very slow, accurate driving but also gives a lot of time to think. The call to do something bigger than farming tugged at me again.

I shut off the tractor, sat back in the seat, and watched a beautiful sunset. The crimson and gold washed over the deep green of the corn and settled beyond the horizon. In the silence, I responded with a plea: "Okay, God, I will give this field of corn to the poor people in Africa. Just let me stay being a farmer."

I did not give that particular year of the crop over to the poor, but several years later, I did and continually do. To this very day, this forty acres is special land for me. The land has now been certified organic for over twenty-five years. It's beautiful, black, loamy/clay soil. The "livestock" in the soil are so plentiful that at times during tilling when I stop and jump off the tractor, the soil is so soft it covers the top of my boots. I really don't claim this land as my own, but I feel honored to be a steward of the land which is really God's land.

The "tug" did not go away.

Our local parish, the Church of St. Nicholas, had a wonderful priest named Fr. Paul Schmelzer whom I really enjoyed. He had many hobbies: ham radio operator, a pilot, and he also rode a motorcycle, which I could really relate to. He put together a parish mission, inviting in some priests that spoke about the gifts of the Holy Spirit. Some people came up to get prayed over; they were overcome by the Holy Spirit and fell to the floor. I had lots of doubts and actually even became a little confused at all this talk about the Holy Spirit. To me, the Holy Spirit was something that I learned about in religious ed classes. It was in my head, but I didn't realize that the Holy Spirit really desires to be alive in my heart and soul. It was the beginning of the Charismatic Movement in the Catholic Church. I had heard people laugh about others being slain in the spirit and make jokes about them.

About a month or so after that mission, I got into the house from the barn around 9:00 p.m. after vacuum cleaning the cows. The cows loved it when I rubbed their backs with the vacuum hose to get all the dirt or small bugs off them. They would sometimes push against me so hard that I couldn't breathe. It made me laugh that they enjoyed it so much. It also would make the cows shine.

After I got cleaned up, I went up to my room and for some reason sat in front of my mirror.

"Holy Spirit, if you are alive, I ask you to come into my life and take over. Come into my heart and soul and fill me."

Not much happened after that. I didn't "feel" any power…but the tug didn't go away. In fact, I started thinking of the priesthood.

Priesthood!

I almost laughed out loud. Me, Mark Stang, this shy, quiet guy, who feels right at home on the soil of the farm—wearing robes and standing up in front of the church. No way!

"God, you've got the wrong guy. I am not near holy enough or smart enough or articulate enough to be a priest!"

The tug continued, ever so slightly. This thought of being a priest kept trickling into my mind. I wanted it to go away: I thought, *You can do greater things for other people.* Farming is a very noble task.

The farmer puts food on the table which is so very important. A farmer has a vital call from God.

Any time the thought of priesthood came to my mind, I started thinking, *Not me. I am not holy enough. I am not smart enough. I am not*—The list went on and on. I kept saying—praying—"God, you've got the wrong guy. It's my brother. He has the personality, the gifts, the…"

I had at one time thought a priest only stayed in the rectory and read books and prayed. But then I thought about Fr. Schmelzer and all his hobbies. He flew airplanes and drove a motorcycle. This priest had the same hobbies as a "normal" person. This gave me the courage to talk to Father Schmelzer.

"Talking" consisted of several conversations without really being able to tell him of the tug. I was too shy and didn't have the courage. He eventually told me about a new retreat called TEC— Teens Encounter Christ. This sounded appealing—a silent retreat (I thought) where I could take time off the farm to think and listen to God in the quiet. I packed a few clothes and my rosary and left for the weekend.

TEC was a life-changing experience for me. It was far from silent, and what I encountered was a powerful sense of God's love for me. Lots of healing happened to me that weekend, especially letting go of past hurts of being called stupid. I also realized how negative I felt about myself. The retreat emphasized God's love for us no matter what. That God's love is endless and His mercy is abundant. All we have to do is open our hearts and accept that mercy and love.

Toward the end of the retreat, I had a powerful moment when we were in our small groups. Each one of us took a turn to hold a hand-sized crucifix and to speak out loud directly to Jesus. This was a very new way of praying for me. This was not rote prayer; this was speaking from the heart and honestly sharing ourselves with Jesus as if he were right there.

The crucifix was blurry as I looked through the tears rolling out of my eyes and falling upon Jesus as I held him in my hands. I prayed aloud: "Jesus, I didn't really realize you love me so deeply. I thank you for the gift of life and now for this great gift of faith that helps me to know that you are real and alive and that you work in my life every day with your abundant love."

I couldn't get any more words out; I just let the tears flow. People in the circle gave me this sacred time just to be supportive of me with Jesus. After a while, I handed the cross over to the next person. I then prayed for the others to have a deep encounter with Christ as I just had.

I was on a high. I didn't know how to go back home, for I felt like such a different person. I felt so lifted up and had a different image of myself. The struggle with low self-esteem had diminished a little. I began to see myself the way God sees me and loves me. How beautiful to reflect that God loves me just as I am—that God made me, and God does not make junk—no matter how much others tried to make me feel like junk.

The tug didn't go away as I had hoped it would when I entered the retreat. In fact, it became stronger despite my great arguments with God: "I could never do that. I get scared in front of five people. I am not smart enough. I just barely made it through high school. I am certainly not holy enough."

Don Wagner, a friend from high school, was on our softball team. He announced that he was going into the seminary. "Yes," I told God. "Don is the kind of guy you want." I asked Don after a game if seminarians have to read the whole Bible. I thought, *There is no way I could do that. I couldn't finish a thirty-page book in high school. God, if you are calling me, you've got the wrong guy. Mike, my brother...*

None of my pleas mattered. The tug was still telling me that I could be doing more. I kept talking to God: "I love to farm. This is me. I am good at it. We are making money. I will give to the poor, just let me stay here where I am comfortable."

Finally, after many months, I told Fr. Paul about the tug. He supported me and directed me to Fr. Johnny Miller, the vocation director of the Diocese of Saint Cloud. I was feeling quite nervous. What are the people going to say when the word gets out? I kept informing Fr. Johnny that I was only going to go into the seminary for six months and then I would be back. I just need to wash this tug out of my system.

In the fall of 1983, after all the fieldwork was done, I left the farm in the care of my cousin, Daryl Stang. I had vacation plans to meet my brother Mike in New York, and we were to fly to Scotland to visit our brother Jeff in the Navy. I figured this would give me some time away to decide whether I really should enter the seminary, for it seemed as if all the doors were opening to it.

We had a wonderful trip. Together we traveled Scotland and England, then took a boat across to France and visited Austria and the Alps. It was one of those very low-budget trips where we bought a loaf of bread and some sausage and ate sandwiches and slept in youth hostels and sometimes under the stars. I did tell Mike and Jeff my thoughts about entering the seminary. They were surprised, but I told them I would go for only six months, and then I would come back to the farm. Only six months, I kept saying. I couldn't even say *seminary*. The words *me* and *seminary* did not belong in the same sentence.

Mike and Jeff were at first surprised, then quiet, then supportive. Both of them said, "Mark, you've got to know what's in your heart, and whatever way you choose, we will support you."

When I came home, I found that Daryl had done a wonderful job with the farm. I felt confident that he could care for the farm while I was away for six months.

Well, the day came when I knew I had to tell Dad and Mom. I couldn't wait any longer. After our lunch one afternoon, when we got done with our final meal prayers, I built up the courage to speak.

"I have something to tell you...I'm thinking about taking time off the farm to enter the seminary for six months."

There was a look of shock in Mom's and Dad's eyes and a moment of silence.

Dad did not respond right away. I knew he was going to need to think about it before he responded. But it made me feel a little uncomfortable. Mom was very surprised and responded, "Well, Mark, you've got to know what you need to do."

I felt both relieved and yet a bit scared of what was about to happen in my future.

The next day at the dinner table, Dad looked me in the eyes and said, "I would be willing to give up half of the farm in order to have a priest in the family." This was a huge statement for Dad to make, knowing how much the farm meant to him, that he would be willing to let go of his dream in order to have a priest in the family. That was his blessing to me. As a son, I did not want to fail my dad, so this blessing was invaluable for me to feel free to go and seek where God was possibly calling me.

Mom was again so supportive as always. A week later, she said, "Mark, you have to know what brings you peace." I told them I was only going to be gone for six months just to get this "out of my system." Dad said, "We can handle it here on the farm with the help of Daryl. You just go and do what you need to do." I felt relieved and yet scared, knowing I really was going to go through with this.

Telling my friends also wasn't easy. When the word got out that night, one of them yelled from the other end of the bar, "Mark, how could you betray us?" He did not know what he was saying. I just wanted to hide at that moment. Religion wasn't something we talked about very often, so I'm sure it made some of my friends uneasy. However, many of them were very supportive of me.

Fr. Johnny Miller, my vocation director, said I had a choice to go either to St. John Vianney Seminary in St. Paul or to Immaculate Heart of Mary Seminary in Winona, Minnesota. I chose Winona because it was a more rural setting. St. Paul was way too big of a pond for this little fish!

I didn't have a car at the time. I couldn't use the farm truck, so Dad was nice enough to let me use his collector car, a 1954 Ford. It was a four-and-a-half-hour ride from the farm to the seminary. After I got through the cities, I found it to be a very beautiful ride down Highway 61. However, it did seem to get longer the closer I got to Winona.

It didn't take long to find out I was not alone. I soon met many other guys who were going through the same feeling I was. One of them was Don Wagner, the softball teammate who had gone into the seminary a few years before me. I also quickly met other farm boys

I could relate to. So even though classes were intimidating and challenging, I had great support in the seminary community.

Lord, at times we are called to step outside of our comfort zone. Thank you for the times in which you send people into our lives to give us support.

Answering the Call

As in all aspects of my life, whatever I do, I am going to give it my all. If I was going to be a priest, I was going to be one of the best priests. I knew I had to do all that I could to earn passing grades in the seminary. I loved all the other activities in the seminary—eating together, praying, and playing my favorite sports. Physically I bloomed to be much stronger and faster than I was in high school. I love team sports, especially volleyball, and enjoyed being on the team.

One of my first classes was logic. The professor, Fr. Fabian, was a brilliant man. He knew every student by name before the first class started. I was always very intimidated by smart people, especially teachers. This guy blew me away. He began the course with a "ten-point quiz" that really wasn't going to affect our grade. He just wanted to see how we would do. Question number two had the word "Socrates," the famous philosopher, in it. It was the first time I had ever seen the word. I knew what a rat was. We have them on the farm. I hesitated, but then I thought, I need to give it my all. So I slowly raised my hand.

"Father Fabian, what is a 'sock-rat' on question number two?"

His eyes grew round, his mouth fell open, and the whole class laughed out loud. This brought back memories of my grade school and middle school years.

It didn't take long before I was advised to go to the tutor's office. I worked with a patient lady who helped me read. She also helped me with my papers and other assignments. One day, I went into her office with a paper I had put a lot of time into. I was sure that I had no mistakes and that everything was grammatically correct. The tutor worked with me for a while. My heart sank as the paper, line after line, was scratched with red ink. She talked about compound sentences and prepositions and many other terms I'm sure I must have learned in high school. Near the end of the paper, she pointed out the word "preisthood." She looked at me and said, "Mark, if you want to be a priest, you first need to learn how to spell the word *priesthood*." I left her office and walked back to my room toward the seminary, believing I was once again in the wrong place.

That day was a beautiful spring day. I knew my dad was out working the field, and I wanted so badly to be home. That's where I needed to be—out in the field on a tractor. I felt like a fish out of water. I was sure that I got it wrong or God got it wrong. He was calling the wrong guy. I was ready to give up. My spiritual director kept encouraging me not to quit, but I knew this priesthood thing was not for me. I told him I needed to leave, but he advised me to stay for the weekend, when a visiting priest would be giving a retreat.

This priest, Fr. Roger Geditz, was from South Dakota. He spoke about being a farm boy and how difficult it was for him to leave the farm and join the seminary. I could really relate to this guy. He shared that when he was in the seminary, he would spend one hour a day before the Blessed Sacrament in quiet prayer. That statement struck me so hard. I thought to myself, *Yes, I need to be silent to be able to listen to what God wants me to do. I will never truly be at peace until I know and do God's will.*

Years later, I remembered hearing about an interview that Dan Rather did with Mother Teresa. He asked, "When you pray, what do you say to God?"

"Nothing, I just listen."

Then Dan Rather asked, "What does God say to you?"

"Nothing, he just listens."

That weekend I made a commitment to stay in the seminary and to make a holy hour each day until the end of the semester.

The next day I started. I remember looking at my watch often, thinking, *Wow, this is a long time to be still.* I remember struggling in later days to get the hour in and fulfill my commitment. The afternoon was the only available time, and I was missing some softball games. This distraction made it difficult for me to listen. The fruit of the prayer was nothing—nothing but silence from God. I remember often asking God, "Just tell me I am not supposed to be a priest."

The semester came to a finish. I was back on the farm. The fish was back in the water!

The tug did not go away. In fact, it slowly grew stronger.

I decided to continue the next fall for another semester, still thinking this tug would leave me. Instead of using my dad's 1954 Ford, I decided to move back to the seminary with my motorcycle. I had my curtains and curtain rod in a box behind me on the back seat, and over the front fender I put my garment bag with my suit coat and all my shirts. The two side saddlebags were packed full of all that I needed.

A year turned into two years, and then Dad said, "Mark, you need to make a decision. Either come home or sell the personal property and cows back to me. The new hired hands are not working out, and things are falling apart. There is a government herd buyout we can enter [because there was too much milk on the market at the time]. If the government accepts our bid, the cows will have to go to slaughter."

I told him, "Submit the bid, and if it's too high, we will keep the cows."

Dad's bid was high, but the bid was accepted, and all the cows went to slaughter. Dad could not tell me this happened; my uncle told me. I was so sad that I cried. I thought of all those bovine personalities, all the good genetics. Those cows were good producers! Most of all, they were like my pets. I remember feeling down and questioning myself. Had I done the right thing? This also was a time that God was able to form me because I was letting go. It was a time that I was weak. I believe that it is in our weakness that God is able to form us. It is in our weakness that we are pliable. When I am strong, I turn lumpy, and God has a hard time forming me. The desire, the tug to be a priest, grew in me as I died to myself. This was a huge step of letting go and trusting.

Please, God, make it clear. Give me a sign that I am doing your will!
Silence.
Nothing.

I did notice one difference at the seminary after I could no longer go back to milking cows. When it was my turn to read aloud, my knees no longer were shaking. It was a night-and-day difference. I am still scared to get up in front of people, but I don't shake. I was wondering if this calmness in front of people was a gift from God. I noticed I started feeling a little more confident about myself.

Immaculate Heart of Mary seminary is located on the campus of St. Mary's University in Winona. In one of my classes, I met a woman named "Wendy," who attended the College of St. Teresa, also in Winona. She had a quiet, shy personality and was very beautiful, not only on the outside; her inner beauty captivated me. As I got to know her, I discovered that she had a great devotion to our Blessed Mother. I felt so comfortable praying with her in the college chapel. My feelings for her grew stronger. That summer, I was asked to stay at the seminary. Fr. Gerald Mahon, otherwise known as Fr. Jerry, the rector of the seminary, said he needed a strong back to help remodel the chapel. The farm was in a quiet "hold" mode as the livestock were gone and we did not rent the extra land. In this summer, I kept in touch with Wendy. She lived right in Winona. Ours was a unique relationship. As I got to know her, she developed a great respect for me, and she had great respect for the priesthood. I believed I was truly falling in love with her.

I brought my feelings to God: *Lord, I know I am not smart enough to be a priest. I am not holy enough. I am not articulate. I could never get up in front of a crowd and talk about God. I could be a good husband, a good father. Could you give me a sign to make this calling more clear?*

The answer was...silence.

Father Mahon was a great mentor to me. I could be so honest with him. I told him about my feelings for Wendy. He knew me well and guided me rather than scolding me. He didn't lock me in and put a wall around me so that I would not have friendships with women. He let me be free to explore possibilities other than the priesthood. He also guided me and encouraged me to talk to God continually, even if I didn't get an answer.

Fr. Jerry also helped me heal from past hurts. In a spiritual direction session, he said, "Mark, if I could only pull your spiritual heart out of your chest and have you see how beautiful it is, and then put it back in, hopefully then you would see how much God loves you." I more and more was able to allow my past hurts to become more of my strength in my weakness.

For example, Fr. Jerry asked me to imagine what my heart looks like. I brought it to prayer, and an image came to mind: a close-up of a small garden—maybe two feet by three feet. The garden was frozen hard. A little snow sat on top, in the midst of dead brown weeds. I saw ice on top of the frozen soil. This to me was the symbol of my low self-esteem. When Fr. Jerry asked why I had such low self-esteem, we explored times in my life when I was hurt.

One of the hurts I shared was Henry and the baseball tryout. Fr. Jerry encouraged me to imagine Henry sitting in front of me in a chair, then speak to Henry and say out loud and sincerely, "Henry, I forgive you." Then I needed to tell Henry how this event hurt me and how I felt.

I did this work. The next day, I shared with Fr. Jerry, "I still felt the anger and resentment."

"Mark, keep doing it. In fact, do this practice every day until it becomes boring."

I took Fr. Jerry's advice. Every day, I sat down and imagined Henry sitting in a chair in front of me. I told him how I felt. After twenty-one days, I was able to say, "This pain is gone: this is boring."

I did this with the other hurts in my life. Through this work of forgiveness, the image of my heart changed. More and more the snow and ice melted. Warm springtime and new life took over until I saw beautiful flowers emerging from the life-giving soft soil.

As I resumed classes, I was again in the tutor's office needing help. I flunked Latin. So then I was encouraged to take Hebrew, which wasn't any easier. My spiritual directors were very helpful; in fact, I met with two of them often.

Falling in love with Wendy—was this God calling me out of the seminary? Meanwhile, my spiritual directors kept pointing me to the priesthood. I saw other seminarians, who I thought would be much better than I, being asked to leave. Why were they asked to leave and not me who was struggling to make the grade? This confused me. I had to believe that God was guiding me through my spiritual directors.

As I finished my years in the minor seminary, I needed to decide where to go for the next four years of study. Several priests advised my vocation director that I would not make the grade at St. John's Seminary in Collegeville in my home diocese. They encouraged me to continue on with my studies at the major seminary of Mount St. Mary's in Emmitsburg, Maryland.

Lord, I find myself praying with my hands closed, fisted, begging you to answer my prayer and give me some kind of sign. Lord, help me to let go and open my hands and completely surrender to your will.

Vision

As I began my second year of major seminary, the assignments and the volume of reading quickly overwhelmed me. I could not comprehend the complex readings. Christology, Canon Law—the words swam on the page. I told myself, "Mark, you need to know this and understand it to pass the test." Only two weeks into the semester, I was far behind my classmates with the requirements the professors were asking of us. All those words, words, words that made sense to everyone else made no sense to me. This brought up even more doubt and now something greater: fear. Like the fourth-grade boy, I was going to fail. Again. This fear made studying even more difficult.

I shared my struggles with each of my spiritual directors, Fr. Anthony Manochio and Fr. Robert Zylla. I was hoping for some message from them that it would be wise for me to discontinue the seminary.

They both encouraged me to continue. They must have seen something in me that I did not see. Father Tony said, "Mark, continue to pray about this, and really ask God to guide you." I had to believe that God was guiding me through these men's encouragement. Still, I was filled with doubt.

My Holy Hour continued as before: Silence. Dryness.

Fr. Zylla said, "Mark, it will come. Just relax. Give it another week." I had great respect for Fr. Zylla. He was a calm, wise man.

One more week.

Nothing changed.

Dryness.

This was too much for me. I knew I could not pass the courses, and I heard nothing from God. I knew then that I needed to leave the seminary. Again, I was the little fourth grader who read at first-grade level, the fifth grader who tried hard to stop the bus but was chastised anyway. Just not good enough. Again—still—I was a fish out of the water.

I knew my family would support me in this decision. And yet, was I letting God down?

Both my directors were understanding and gave me their blessing. I packed up my things and prepared to leave. I told only my closest friends who knew of my struggles. They understood and felt bad that I was going to leave them but encouraged me to do what my heart felt most at peace doing.

On Saturday morning, all of my personal belongings were packed into my red 1984 Subaru Outback. I was ready to head back home. To what? I wasn't sure, but I knew it wasn't going to be the seminary. I had decided to visit my brother Mike and his family in New Hampshire on the way home, to get a little breathing time and figure out what I was going to do with myself now that seminary was behind me.

A Mass was being held at 6:30 that morning for those who were leaving early for their apostolic ministry for the day. I wanted to attend, as a sort of final blessing send-off before I departed. The Mass was held in the seminary chapel—the place I had spent many hours in quiet prayer. About thirty men were present. Fr. Manochio was the main celebrant of the Mass.

I have to confess that my mind was everywhere but on the Mass. I didn't hear the Scripture readings. I didn't see the consecration of the Holy Eucharist. I was physically present, but I wasn't present in my mind. Mostly, I was thinking of how to navigate around New York City to get to Mike's place.

I walked up for communion. The instant the Body of Christ touched my tongue, my legs became weak. I lost all strength.

This is unusual for me. Am I fainting? I don't feel sick. But this is so powerful. I can't hold myself up.

I wobbled along until I almost fell over, catching myself on the front pew. When I got around and into the pew, I knelt down right there, put my head into my hands, and prayed, "Lord, what is happening?" I did not feel frightened. In fact, a strong sense of peace flowed over me.

As the rest of the seminarians came forward to receive communion, I lifted my head and looked toward the altar.

There I saw...

A silhouette...

I saw myself, vested as a priest...with my hands together... reaching high...elevating the Body of Christ as priests do as part of the consecration of the Eucharist.

In an instant, it was gone.

What had I just seen?

Tears came down my cheeks as I knelt there in utter astonishment.

For a long time, I could not say anything. I hoped for a message or even some voice to speak to my heart to give me some clarity on this vision. But there was nothing but silence.

"Lord," I prayed, "how can I be your priest? I can't do it. I'm not smart enough. I'm not good enough. I'm just not—enough. I want to leave. I *need* to leave."

I knew that something supernatural had happened. A waterfall of—something.

I sat in that front pew for two more hours, at times just sobbing deeply. I was crying out all my feelings—all the anguish, all the uncertainty, all the insecurity, and especially all the fear.

What is happening? Did I really see that?

Then I noticed that the chapel was being prepared for another Mass, so I needed to step out.

I walked out the chapel door, took a deep breath, and walked slowly outside to my car. I pondered again.

Then grabbed some items and went back to my room.

Lord, tell me—what am I supposed to do?

I received no answer. All I knew is that something supernatural had happened.

And so I changed my mind and unpacked my car.

I went to my classmate who still had all my books that he was going to return for me. I didn't explain in detail; I just said to him and my other friends that something had happened, and I couldn't explain it. He and all the others were supportive and understanding and said they would pray for me.

Back in my room, I looked at that stack of books and picked up one about two inches thick.

Lord, You're really going to have to help me.

I told my spiritual directors that something just happened but I couldn't explain it. They smiled and welcomed me to continue.

Lord, at times You manifest yourself in special ways: In the Eucharist. In the sacraments. In nature. In one another. Some large, some small. Open my eyes, open my ears, open my heart. Make me ready for an encounter with You.

"Be still and know that I am God" (Psalm 46:10).

"Are You Weak Enough?"

I continued in the seminary. My instructors passed me because they knew I was trying—just like minor seminary. The more I learned about the priesthood, the more inadequate I felt.

The fish out of the water.

Because holy hour was so quiet, I did most of the "talking." This is often what I would say to the Lord in the quiet of my heart: *How could I ever be a priest? I'm not smart enough. I'm certainly not holy enough. I'm not articulate like my classmates. I am afraid of speaking to the crowds. I could be a good husband and father. God, what is your plan for me? O God, I just want to do your will.*

My holy hours after that vision were the same as before. Quiet. Silent. Dry.

Bishop Paul Dudley, from the Dioceses of Sioux Falls, South Dakota, gave a talk to all the seminarians in which he said, "Are you weak enough to be a priest?" This struck me. Am I weak enough to be a priest?

Was I looking at this the wrong way? I felt I had to be much better than I was to be one of God's priests. I had to be smart, holy, articulate. Was I running on the energy of pride? If God is calling me, then Mark Stang has to be *his* best. He—Mark—has to shine. He has to be good so that others can think well of him—so that God can think well of him.

Yuck! What kind of life is that?

Wanting to be the best—that was pride. But being "weak enough"…this was a whole new way of seeing. I came to understand that the healthy way of "being the best" was simply surrendering and finding my call.

I find it so difficult to acknowledge that I am a vulnerable person. But when I do, I find myself more relaxed and open to new changes in my life. I truly grow and become the person God has created me to become.

In scripture, we read, "Yahweh, you are our Father; we the clay and you our potter, all of us are the work of your hands" (Isaiah 64:7). I realize I am that ball of clay in the hand of God. When I look back on my life, I see times in my life when that ball was hard and crumbly, and God could not do anything with it. But when I realized how weak I am and allowed myself to become vulnerable, my clay became soft and pliable in the hands of God. It is then that God can take me and create me to be a beautiful instrument for His work.

Lord, I pray for strength to be weak to be strong in You. Help me to die to my pride and let go of my control.

At midyear of my third year, it was time to set the Diaconate ordination date with the bishop. I followed protocol and traveled back to St. Cloud to Bishop Jerome Hanus's office to ask him if he would accept me for ordination.

In his office, we talked about farming. We talked about the weather and sports. Finally, he said, "Well, Mark, aren't you going to ask me if I will ordain you?"

"Ahh…yeah, I guess I am going to ask you."

"Well, from the reports that I got from your formation directors, I know you struggle with academics. But what I know of you… yes, I will ordain you." We set the date for June 17, 1990.

After the meeting, I thought I should be happy because this was like proposing marriage to my girlfriend. But I was not excited. I was so uncertain. Even though I had grown and healed and learned so much, the tug was slight. I did want to do God's will, but I felt inadequate and unsure, especially about whether I could handle the celibacy, for I wanted to get married.

Could I live a life of celibacy? Could I live without a partner? Without someone to physically hold me? This means I had to give up the dream of having my own children and being a father to them.

Classes started up again in January of 1990 in Maryland at "The Mount."

One day during one of my holy hours, I thought, *Time is getting close. I really need to make a decision.* I decided to just crack open the Bible to get some kind of message from God. The Bible opened to James 1:6 which says, "But the prayer must be made with faith, and no trace of doubt because a person who has doubts is like the waves thrown up in the sea by the buffeting of the wind." Indeed, I *had* been tossing around on waves of doubt, a little fish in tumultuous water. I believe this was meant for me to make a commitment and no longer be vacillating.

At that moment, I realized that God was *inviting* me to the priesthood, not *forcing* me. It was a choice that was up to me. He was inviting, and I could choose either way. Whichever I chose, He would be there with me. I believe God gives us freedom. If I chose to leave and get married, He would be there and bless me. The same if I chose the priesthood. I thought for a while and decided, *Lord, the world needs priests. I will be one of your priests.*

I took a deep breath.

Okay, Lord, here we go.

Still I felt inadequate to make this commitment.

Lord, I can only do this by the power of Your grace.

As I left the chapel that day, I encountered my friend Peter and said, "Peter, guess what? Today I decided to be a priest!"

Peter smiled, as he knew I was struggling in my discernment.

After that decision, the doubts only intensified.

Who do you think you are?

You are not smart enough.

You are not holy enough.

You will never be able to—

and on and on.

Then I realized…these thoughts can't be coming from God. I knew that I struggled with low self-esteem. I came to understand that these negative voices were not from God. If God was calling me, He would not be giving me messages of doubt.

I tried not to give the evil one any attention. I dismissed the thoughts as fast as I could. In my mind, I was saying, "Satan, begone," and then repeating, "Jesus, Jesus."

This was exhausting at times because, in a little while, the thoughts crept back. Many times during the day, Satan reminded me of how unfit I was to be a priest. I saw little confirmation that I had made the right decision.

My holy hours were the same: dry and silent. I seemed even more distracted by self-doubt. The litany kept playing over and over: You are not good enough, you will never be able. Again and again, like waves. I thought, *Stupid Mark is out of his league.*

I really had to put faith in my spiritual directors, who insisted, "There is something in you." I kept thinking, "Well, I sure don't see it. What am I doing here? I want to go back to the farm. I knew what I was doing back home. The farm is where I was successful. I belong there, not here."

In February 1990, we held a five-day diaconate retreat right at the seminary. In the retreat, I wanted to deal with the conflict I felt inside of me. I spent many hours in silence, but the silence was not in me. Instead, I felt so much turmoil. In the years of my formation, we had talks on celibacy. Some made sense; others were difficult for me to grasp. I realized during the retreat that things were coming closer to the final decision.

Can I really go through with this? Am I really called? God, You are so quiet. I hear nothing from You, and yet I am supposed to follow You. At least the Apostles had someone to look at, to actually hear, to touch. All I get is this small tug on the heart and lots of silence. All I can do is to have courage and to trust that this is what You want. For I want what You desire.

At the end of the retreat, I was still in turmoil. I had spent most of the day in a quiet place in the college chapel. I had hoped that if I gave more time to silent prayer, God would finally "give in" and send me some kind of sign. But instead…

Nothing.

I left the chapel and headed to my room. It was late at night, far past my normal bedtime. As I walked past the seminary chapel, I felt a desire to stop in for one quick visit before going to bed.

No one was inside. I walked all the way up to the tabernacle and knelt down. I opened my arms and said in my heart, *Lord, I surrender. I give all that I am to You—all that I have: My gifts. My talents. My money. My sexuality. I give my life to You. I just want to unite my heart with your Sacred Heart on the cross.*

Cold darkness came over me. I had an image in my mind of a face coming from my right side, breaking through skin-like walls. Not a pretty face...not like anyone I would recognize...a mean, angry man's face. He had large ears and a large mouth. Behind the face looked like space. Dark.

In the coldness, I heard a voice: "You can't. You are not good enough. You are not capable because of your past sins."

I realized then that this was Satan, and so I prayed, "Satan, begone!"

"Satan, begone!"

Many times I prayed it. Over and over, like waves.

I thrust my right hand as to push the evil one away.

The coldness faded away.

After a moment a warm, white light washed over me.

From in front of me, I heard a much softer, kinder voice: "Do you realize what you are asking?"

And then...silence...

What had just happened?

I want to unite my heart with the Sacred Heart of Jesus on the cross.
Wow.

Then another seminarian walked into the chapel. I got up and moved to the statue of Mary and asked her to show me and to prepare me to unite my heart with the Heart of Jesus. In praying this, I disposed myself to God by surrendering myself totally to his will. I gave everything I have over to him.

God, help me to always dispose myself totally to You because I desire to unite my will with Yours, to unite my heart with Your Sacred Heart of Jesus. I do this through the one person who did it and wants to show us and lead us to You, O Jesus, and that is our Mother Mary. Mary, I consecrate my life to you. All that I am and have. Lead me, guide me, show me the way to the Sacred Heart of Jesus.

I consecrated my commitment to the Immaculate Heart of Mary.

Jesus, Mary, Joseph, help me in this commitment.

The silence, the dryness in my prayer, was lifted in a powerful way for a moment. I almost had to pinch myself. Did that really happen? A spirit of peace replaced the cloud of doubt in me.

Thank you, God. Be near me now and always. I love You, and I know You love me.

A New Kind of Weakness

Afterward, in my silent prayer, I wanted to spend more time in thanksgiving.

In the following week, though, doubts returned to bother me. My childhood years came back to mind. I asked for healing from the times I got bullied on the school bus when I was in fourth, fifth, and sixth grades. These were the years my self-image was damaged.

I asked God to pull out that hurt and anger by the roots and fill it with the Holy Spirit. This constant work took many different prayer sessions with God the Healer. More and more with the help of the Holy Spirit, I could let this low self-esteem pain go.

I continued to ponder giving of my whole self totally to God: Could I look at celibacy in a different light? Could I see celibacy as a gift, not another hurdle? Could I live out what they tell me—that celibacy *frees* one to devote oneself totally to God?

My holy hour became less confusing and more focused on listening to what was next: finishing the semester and preparing for ordination to the diaconate. Each day I was more and more able to let go of the doubts, more and more able to walk with confidence and trust that God would provide.

That confidence came through as we had a class on preaching. I spent many hours preparing my first homily in front of my classmates. I spoke about the grace of God and how God wants to spread that grace out from us to others, like a manure spreader.

I thought I did a wonderful job with this homily…only to find that I was quickly criticized. One of my classmates was appalled that I had used the word "manure" from the pulpit. The old feelings of rejection started to well up in me until the professor spoke up with a story of President Truman: During his speech, a woman sitting beside the First Lady whispered to her, asking if she could have the president not use the word "manure" when he talked. Mrs. Truman whispered back, "You don't know how long it took me to get him to use the word 'manure' instead of what he was using." Everyone had a good laugh. This was huge for me. Farmboy Mark could still be himself and be a priest. I felt at peace and supported in following where my heart was leading rather than following the "norm," or "making the grade," or worrying about being accepted. If I could minister more from the heart rather than from the head, I *could* be a priest.

One day in March, I noticed a lump in my abdomen. It was not on the surface, but when I pushed down under the skin near my belly button, I could feel something hard. I ignored it because it wasn't painful. I wasn't feeling sick. In fact, I was feeling pretty strong. That week, I had even hit a lucky home run at the college intramural softball game.

After a week or so, the lump was not going away; rather, it was increasing. I went to see the college nurse, and she had me see the doctor a few days later. He suggested that I see the local doctor. When I met him, I got an uneasy feeling. He was not very professional and lacked bedside manner. He kept saying, "This is not a good place." When he felt the lump, he said, "Yes, that is not normal. Come back tomorrow, and we will put you under the knife and see what it is." To say the least, this made me feel quite uncomfortable. I needed a second opinion.

That afternoon, I scheduled an appointment with St. Agnes Hospital in Baltimore, Maryland, to seek another opinion. I was bummed because I had to schedule the appointment on the same day we had a very important softball game. I had two of my good friends from the seminary go with me: Marty Schafer and Mark Lichter. They could make me laugh, and we were having a good time.

I underwent a CT scan, and we waited for what felt like hours in the waiting room for the doctor to call me in. The waiting room was quiet, and a feeling of tension hung over us. Marty and Mark made such a difference; Mark could imitate one of our professors so accurately and make us laugh, and when one holds back a laugh so not to let others know, it makes one want to laugh all the more. We tried to be quiet in respect of the others, but I don't know how well we succeeded. Other patients kept being called into the doctor's office before me, and I was not called in until the end. Finally my name was called; I had Mark and Marty wait in the waiting room.

When I got into the office, I understood why I was called last. The doctor looked at me with compassion and concern.

"Mark, you have a tumor, and we believe it could very likely be cancer."

The news hit me like a punch in the gut.

The doctor was very good in explaining the situation. He said, "We notice on the CAT scan that there is a tumor in your abdomen the size of a small football. It is connected to your mesentery track, which is a lining that holds up your stomach. It is a lymphoma type of cancer. We need to do an operation to do a biopsy to determine more and to see what type of chemotherapy or radiation to use."

I asked, "Can't you just remove it all?"

The doctor said, "No, this type of cancer is throughout your body in all of your lymph glands. You may want to think about this. We can do the procedure here or send you to Johns Hopkins Hospital, or you may want to do this in your home state at the Mayo Clinic in Rochester, Minnesota."

I was glad the doctor gave me a chance to think about it and that I didn't need to have an answer right away. When I heard the words *Mayo Clinic*, I knew that would be a good safe place to go if I could get in for an appointment.

Mark and Marty were so good waiting in the now-empty waiting room. They were still in a laughing mood. It must have been because we seldom got out of the seminary, and this was one of those breaks we needed. When we got into the elevator, I said, "Guys, I have cancer."

Saying those words for the first time made my heart sink faster than the elevator was taking us down those eight floors. Mark and Marty reacted with shock, sadness, and support. We stopped to eat on the way home, for we had not had anything to eat since breakfast. However, I was not hungry. So many things were going through my mind: *Is this true? Can it be? What do I say to my family?*

I kept thinking of the word.

Cancer.

When Fr. Jerry Mahon heard the news, he said, "Mark, I can get you in to see a Mayo specialist ASAP. You can stay here with me in Winona. It is a forty-five-minute drive." The move to Winona was easy. The directors at The Mount were so helpful, and the rector of the seminary helped me so much. He left me a note and said I could help myself to his personal refrigerator, and whatever I needed I should just contact him. He also said he and all the guys in the seminary would be praying for me.

With more tests and a CT scan at the Mayo Clinic, the doctors confirmed the reality. I had a fast-growing non-Hodgkin's lymphoma.

I actually was blessed with two doctors: Dr. Thomas Witzig and a doctor who was studying under him, Dr. Timothy Call. The next day, I was put into surgery for a biopsy, and they had to lay my intestinal tract out on a table beside me. They did not remove the whole tumor, for it was linked to my entire lymphatic system. I was then admitted to Methodist Hospital—a room on the sixth floor.

After the shock of learning I had cancer, I was overwhelmed by all that I had to do and go through including the surgery. I was scared and confused. What was happening? *Why* was it happening? After all my years of struggling with the call to the priesthood, why was God drowning me in yet another struggle? *Why?*

Next, the doctors wanted to do a bone marrow biopsy. They explained that they were going to drill into the center of the back of my hip to get some marrow. They could numb the skin, but there was going to be some pain when they drilled. It was Holy Week. In fact, my procedure day was Good Friday. I thought I could unite my pain with Jesus on the cross. Little did I know how painful it would be.

I was positioned on my side for the bone marrow biopsy procedure. Right in front of me hung a button on a cord. The doctors told me I could push the button whenever I needed to, and it would give me an injection of morphine into my IV that would help ease the pain. I was warned that the morphine took time to work, so I should push the button sooner rather than later when I was in pain. It was as if I was in control of my pain. It makes one ponder—what if we were in that much "control" of all the different pains in our lives?

At first, I thought I wouldn't need this; I have Jesus. But I soon learned how weak I was. I had a metal crucifix the size of my palm, and I could hold it and put my fingers over the corpus of Jesus. In the other hand, I held the button that controlled the morphine. At first, I was doing okay when the needle of Novocain was inserted in me, and they cut my skin open, but as soon as I heard the drill motor and the pressure of the drill bit into the middle of my hip, I started rapidly pushing that button.

The next step was chemotherapy. A dose consisted of five different types of chemo—four with IVs and one taken orally. It would take three to four hours to let the chemo drip into my veins. The doctor said I would be quite sick the first week, then I would level out the next week, and in the third week, I would regain my strength. Then they would give me another dose. I would need to do this six times, three weeks apart.

Getting the chemotherapy wasn't difficult, but as I left the clinic, I already felt nauseated. I could not stop throwing up. I needed a bag as I was traveling from the Mayo Clinic to St. Casimir's Parish in Winona, where Fr. Jerry Mahon was now pastor. He invited me to stay with him after each chemo infusion until I could get my strength back.

When I started my second round, I thought my body would be able to take the chemo with fewer side effects, but I was wrong. The effects were the same. It got to the point where I had nothing to throw up but the mucus that my stomach produced to digest the food.

I spent my time mainly in isolation. Television was just noise. It did not interest me. What was going on in the world, I had no concern for. I went out for walks alone. I found a beautiful spot along the Mississippi River where I could sit and watch the water flow. I could put my cares and fears into the water and let them flow away downriver. I also spent time in the chapel, asking God many questions. In return...silence.

Fr. Jerry Mahon was a great nurse to have as I recovered. He got me all I needed, but most especially he listened to me. I needed that because I cried a lot. Crying comes easily for me. I guess it is a gift because I always feel better after a cry. I think I got the gift of crying from my father's side. I think it's healing. I just have to drink that much more water!

I went back home to the farm in my third week after the second round of chemo. We had a family gathering; I don't remember the occasion, but some of my siblings from out of state were home. I didn't realize until later how the cancer affected them, especially Mom and Dad. They had been at my bedside as I was recovering at Methodist Hospital in Rochester. How much pain they were going through! To see their son who was to take over the farm, then leave and discern to be a priest, now dying of cancer. I believe oftentimes there is more pain outside the hospital bed than inside the hospital bed. The pain is called love. Thank you, Mom and Dad and family and friends. Thank you for the love.

My sister Stacie shaved my head because what I was warned about came true—my hair did fall out. It came out first in the comb and then in the shower—gobs of it at a time. This was another step into the reality of how fragile my body had become. I was scared. I realized I could die. People said I looked good with no hair, but I often think about how difficult it must be for a woman to lose her hair.

I discussed with the bishop my upcoming diaconate ordination in June, which was only a month away. He spoke about my paperwork from the seminary that had to be completed. The seminary sent me my master's degree. This was truly a gift as it was given to me without my needing to finish the spring semester. I had forgotten about all that academic work until the bishop told me. Thank you, Mount St. Mary's.

The vision of the man's face and then the bright light with a voice that said, "Do you know what you are asking?"—and now this suffering. I believe this is all part of uniting my will with Yours, Jesus.

And all the people praying for me—may You return their prayers a hundredfold, and may all who pray for me be united closer as a family with their own and as a family in unity with You.

Amazingly, I don't have much anxiety about this cancer. I still have more anxiety for my ordination than this illness. God, help me to learn from this illness. I offer up all my suffering and unite it with Your suffering on the cross. Help me to love You more and to give Your love to others more. Help me to focus not on myself but on others.

Darkness and Light

We had to move the diaconate ordination date back one week so that I could be ordained in my "third week" when I had the most strength. It was set for June 24, 1990. Bishop Hanus could not be present for the ordination because he was hosting a USCCB Bishops conference at St. John's University in Collegeville, Minnesota. Bishop Hanus asked retired bishop of St. Cloud, Bishop George Speltz, to preside. Bishop Hanus told me he would ask his brother bishops to pray for me. Wow—a group of bishops praying for me. I felt honored.

Bishop Speltz did a wonderful job. Bishop Vlazny from Winona also had made the trip to St. Nicholas for the celebration. My family members from out of state all came home for the occasion. I also had classmates and friends who traveled the long way to be present for me.

I remember saying yes to five questions pertaining to the vows that each transitional deacon is required to take during the ordination ceremony, beyond all the promises of obedience. I knew the question was coming for the vow of celibacy. That question was a big one for me: my "yes" to that question was not as strong as my "yes" to the other questions.

Lord, you are going to have to help me with this commitment.

At the end of the ceremony, I was asked by the bishop to say a few words to the congregation. I said to the people who filled the church, "I know you are praying for me, and I thank you so much for your prayers. Everything is going to be all right." I felt I could say this only because of what happened during my retreat when I united my heart with the Sacred Heart of Jesus on the cross. I chose not to share that intimate moment, but in the back of my mind, I knew that with trust, I *was* going to be all right.

The next morning I was in the Mayo Clinic getting my fourth of six chemotherapy treatments. The first thing was a CT scan to see how the treatments were working. After the CT scan, instead of doing the infusion, I was sent to my doctor's office to wait.

My doctor informed me the scan showed that the main tumor had shrunk in size a little; however, three new tumors had appeared.

"What?"

I was shocked and saddened. I knew I wasn't feeling 100 percent, but I was really counting on the chemo being more effective. I became really scared.

Because of the cancer being aggressive, the doctors recommended chemo plus radiation to the point where I would need a bone marrow transplant. This would require being in isolation for weeks because of my weakened immune system.

"There is a risk to this procedure: You may not make it through," said Dr. Witzig.

I asked, "What are the other options?"

"Well, none really. We could keep you on the chemo only, but we have you on the maximum dosage already. If we don't do anything, it is hard to say how long you can live. It is a fast-growing cancer. You may live a year. Maybe less."

I felt as if I were in a dream. Could this be happening?

I needed time to think about this. My doctor was so understanding and compassionate. I had a few days while they sought a bone marrow donor.

It was very, very difficult calling all my family members and updating them with the new diagnosis. I also called my bishop, Jerome Hanus. I could hear their hearts drop as they became silent on the other end of the phone. That night I went to stay with Fr. Jerry Mahon again.

After the shock of hearing this new diagnosis, my prayer changed.

God, if You are real, why would You do this to me? I thought You needed priests. I thought I gave my life to You. What more do You want, God?

I didn't care to eat. I really didn't care to talk to anyone. When I spent time reflecting on what was happening, I went into a time of deep darkness, surrounded by black. I started wondering: Is there a God?

There was no answer to my questions.

I sank into doubt.

"I think I got brainwashed. Those people who are atheists must be right. What kind of God would be so mean?"

I could feel myself falling into more and more darkness as if someone had pulled the rug out from under me. At the time, when I usually prayed, I didn't feel like going to the chapel to do my holy hour. I told myself, "What's the use?"

But I went. Where else was I to go?

I would just sit there in the silence, close my eyes, and feel the darkness.

Day after day with little consolation.

I did receive an immense amount of sympathy from those who visited me. Their words were very kind. Mom and Dad and other family members and friends would travel from St. Cloud down to Rochester to visit and support me. But deep down, I struggled.

God...where are You?

One day, I sat in the darkness with my eyes closed, trying to find some glimmer of hope. Way, way off in the distance, I noticed a tiny beacon of light. I had to convince myself that the light was Jesus. And then all I could do was try to keep my eye on that tiny light, which at times would fade away.

God, what do You want from me?

Is undergoing the chemo doing God's will?

I feel as if I am with Jesus in the first sorrowful mystery.

If possible, let this cup pass me by—but not my will but Thy will be done.

My emotions were all over the place. At times I felt abandoned—God pulled everything out from under me. I felt afraid, questioning God—why? I even would ask myself, "Should I even question God? Is that wrong of me?" I wondered if it was because of the sin in my life. Maybe God was angry with me.

I would think back to what had happened back in February during my diaconate retreat when I prayed in front of the Blessed Sacrament and united my heart to the Sacred Heart of Jesus on the cross.

Could all this be the answer to my prayer of giving everything over to God?

Surrender—that's what I need to do—just totally surrender every-thing over to God. I thought I did that, but now I have to surrender my whole life over to God.

Surrender

Before I met again with the doctors, I went back home to the farm. Bishop Hanus came to be with me and my parents. I remember a long conversation in the living room. In the end, we all held hands, the bishop leading us in prayer and ending with the Our Father. During that visit, we decided to try to see if my priesthood ordination could happen before I underwent the bone marrow transplant. That way, if I did not survive the cancer, I at least would die a priest. The bishop suggested the idea and said that he would try to get permission from the Vatican in Rome. I was to ask my doctors at the Mayo how long I could postpone the procedure.

The next day, I traveled back to the Mayo clinic and met with my doctors. Instead of stepping right into the treatment, I asked my doctor for three months without treatment to give me time to prepare for my ordination. Dr. Witzig stated, "Waiting that long without treatment is not a good idea."

"How about two months?"

"Mark, the tumor is growing fast, and it is pressing against the tubes going to your kidney."

"How about a month and a half?"

He knew how important this was to me, so we decided that I would return to the Mayo Clinic on the morning of the 28th of August. This meant a full two months without any treatment, which was a serious risk. I have great respect for all doctors, especially my oncologist, Dr. Witzig. I would not recommend postponing treatment to anyone.

The doctors promised to have everything ready for radiation and chemo and a bone marrow transplant. No treatment was given to me; I was just to be back on the 28th to begin the treatment.

I informed Bishop Hanus and my family, and the date set for my ordination was Saturday the 25th of August. My first Mass would be the following day, and then I would travel to the Mayo. My family did all the work in planning the big events—mostly my sister Jean. They just asked a few questions of me once in a while. What a blessing to know that all these people were making this happen for me.

I started to reflect on all that I had been through since the beginning of my calling. All that I had to let go of. All the questioning. All the struggle. And then a thought came to my mind—what I learned about the priesthood and the power of the Eucharist. If I could just celebrate one Mass with these hands of mine and experience the change of bread into the body of Christ and wine into the blood of Christ, just one time, it would all be worth it.

Then, again I sank into deep darkness. I felt so abandoned, so lost. I was falling with the bottom pulled out from under me and only darkness all around. I remember asking God "why" many times and in many ways.

God, why are You taking me from this life, from my family, from my loved ones? I thought You needed priests! All that I had to give up and go through and now this! I am so young. Why, God, why?

There was no answer, no consolation.

I started to think again that this whole God thing was just a hoax. Was I brainwashed into thinking there was someone—some spirit—out there?

I refused to fill up the time with noise; I knew I could not find any answers on the television. I stayed in the silence, waiting. I wasn't sure what I was waiting for but just waited in the dark silence.

The emptiness was painful and scary. Again I heard the words of consolation from my family and friends. I replied to them with a thank you, but nothing anyone said seemed to be the answer.

That tiny spot of light off in the distance. I had nowhere to go, so I had to believe that the small beacon was Christ. I had to force myself to believe that in this emptiness, God was still there.

One morning, outside the window of the chapel I could hear a bird…a mourning dove. The sound of *coo-coo* brought me some peace that I was going to be all right.

I started to pray more with open hands rather than closed fists. My prayer grew from pleading with God to surrendering to God.

I came to really appreciate Fr. Jerry Mahon. He couldn't really give me any answers either, but he encouraged me to think about what heaven is like. I had to take that step in faith and believe, even though I didn't feel anything. I had to believe there must be a God, a higher power, and greater knowledge than I. I didn't understand, but I chose to trust in this Being that I didn't see, this great knowledge. I desired to grow in this knowledge.

I did have a few glimpses of consolation. One time in silence when I closed my eyes, I wanted so much to see Jesus. In the power of my imagination, I got a picture in my mind of the Sacred Heart of Jesus with his arms open and wearing a long white robe. These words came to me: "Just trust in me."

Another consoling moment was when I was asking our Blessed Mother to guide me, and I felt a weakness so much that I couldn't run the rosary beads through my fingers. Again in the power of my imagination, I pictured Mary. She had my rosary in her hand, moving the beads for me. These were not visions I had, but just the gift of my imagination.

I started to focus my energy more on heaven and less on this world. Fr. Jerry said, "What about just accepting you are going to die? Think of heaven and what heaven is like." He helped me think of heaven. I entered even more into a spirit of surrender—surrender to the will of God. Giving everything over.

During this time I wondered often what it would be like being with Jesus in the Garden of Gethsemane.

Lord, let this cup pass me by. But not my will but Your will be done.

Heaven has to be a beautiful place.

I practiced as a deacon at the parish of the Immaculate Conception in Rockville. The pastor's name was Fr. Bob Rolfes. He was a wonderful and understanding priest.

At Immaculate Conception, a lady named Tilly wanted to write an article about me in the local newspaper. I agreed. She asked me many questions, and I answered them as honestly as I could. A day after that article was published, I received another call from the *St. Cloud Times*. Then after a few weeks, there was a call from the *Minneapolis Tribune*. The word of my cancer and ordination kept spreading.

I was uncomfortable with the publicity. However, I also felt wonderful to know that my story was touching many people. I felt, "Who am I, the simple farm boy, with all this attention coming my way?" Still, I felt okay because more people were praying for me. I needed all the prayers I could get. People needed to know my story— or as I often said, God's story.

I also got advice from people about healing remedies: shark cartilage. Juicing carrots. All kinds of supplements. When people would offer me a particular remedy, I would always ask, "Are there any negative side effects?" My thoughts always were, what have I got to lose? So I would try different remedies, even though oftentimes they didn't taste very good.

The ordination date was approaching, and I asked Fr. Jerry to give the homily at my first Mass. He agreed, but the next day he came to me.

"Mark, I prayed about it, and I think you should preach at your first Mass. I will preach at your funeral."

I thought that was a good idea.

Wow, this is really going to happen.

The Poor Clares (an order of nuns) in Sauk Rapids, Minnesota, hosted me during my retreat prior to the priesthood ordination. They were a constant reminder to me of all the people praying for me. In response I kept praying, "Lord, please bless all the people praying for me back a hundredfold in return."

While on retreat, I wrote some reflections in my journal:

> Many, many people have been praying for me, and I feel graced and lifted up.
>
> I am prepared to die. I know of God's mercy because I am a sinner, but God has mercy on me. Thank You, Jesus, for teaching me this important lesson. Help me to know what to say to others to bring them and me to a better understanding of Your will. Give me the strength and courage to fulfill Your will. Praised be Jesus.
>
> I struggle with pride—now I am weak, I am poor, but for some reason I have not lost hope; in fact, the virtue of hope, which I feel is a grace from God stemming from everyone's prayers, is overflowing. Thank You, Jesus.
>
> God, help me to know that You are with me, You are in me, You are the source of all that I am. You wrote that article in the *St. Cloud Times*, not me or not the author, John DuBois.
>
> Touch people's lives so that they may be converted closer to You and that there may be some vocation to the priesthood and religious life.
>
> I am going to do the homily for my first Mass. I ask You, O God, to speak through me. Please send down the Holy Spirit that I may say what You want the people to hear, God.

*****

August 25, 1990, was a hot Saturday. The St. Cloud Cathedral was full. With such short notice, I was so surprised and overwhelmed by the number of priests who came. Many people from out of state and as far east as from the seminary in Emmitsburg, Maryland, came to my ordination.

During the ceremony, the bishop places hands on the deacon for ordination to the priesthood. During that special moment, I felt a warmth washing over me when Bishop Hanus laid his hands on my head. I felt overwhelmed with love and support as the priests took turns placing their hands on my head as well. After the celebration, I tried to greet all the people to thank each one personally for coming. I could not keep the smile off my face. I was on a spiritual high.

This smile ran into the next day which was also a very hot day in the large church in my hometown of St. Nicholas, Minnesota. Here is where I celebrated my first Mass. The church is sometimes called a cathedral in the prairie.

As we began Mass, I felt a heaviness over the crowd. How else should one feel when attending a Mass that could be the last Mass with the main celebrant?

In the homily, I thanked the people for praying for me: "We need to celebrate! You are praying for a miracle. The miracle has taken place. I don't know if it took place in my physical body, but it took place in my heart, in my soul, the important part of me that will live on forever.

"My body will die someday. This cancer that I have I do not wish on anyone. However, I see it as a gift because it gave me the gift of weakness—the gift of brokenness so that I can die to myself and let Christ be the Spirit in me, let Christ be the priest in me. I struggle with the sin of pride. I know my ego gets in the way of the Holy Spirit working in me. I struggle with being in control. This cancer gave me no choice but to let go and let God take over my life. So it is not so much Mark Stang being the priest, but Christ being the priest in me. It is not so much Mark Stang living, but the Spirit living in me. I know many of you are sad, but we need to celebrate!"

At this Mass, I was overwhelmed with emotions. So many people came to support me and pray for me. This certainly was a Mass of gratitude and thanksgiving. But also in the back of my mind, I was thinking, this is going to be the last Mass I have with a large group of people before I go into isolation and possibly not come out. However, the love and support of the people lifted me out of those heavy but real thoughts. My heart was filled with joy in celebrating the priesthood.

The reception served close to 700 people. There were so many good people from St. Nicholas who were willing to give so much. They served chicken and dressing and homemade pies.

One of my good friends who surprised me was Wendy, my friend whom I met in the seminary and who had quietly supported me all through the major seminary. I was so happy to see her come to the celebration. I felt loved and supported by her. Still, I felt sad that our lives would be going in different directions. Her path: marrying another teacher, and together they have eight wonderful children whom they homeschool.

Lord, I am in awe over so many people who gave of their time and energy to pray for me and all those that still do pray for me. Please bless each one with a hundredfold blessings back to them in return.

More to Do

On Monday afternoon, I returned to the Mayo Clinic. I was reflecting on all that had happened over the weekend. What a great celebration! However, my stomach became nauseated as I came over the hill and saw the skyline of Rochester. This wasn't the first time that I had had that bad taste of chemo in my teeth even before the infusion started.

The joy in my heart was mixed with wondering if I was going to survive the bone marrow transplant.

As before, I stayed with Fr. Jerry. Early Tuesday morning, a friend of his dropped me at the clinic. I didn't invite any family or friends to be with me. I didn't want to inconvenience anyone. Plus I needed some time alone.

It wasn't until I became a hospital chaplain that I came to understand that this was not the wisest decision. From *The Four Things That Matter Most: A Book About Living* by Ira Byock, M.D., I learned:

> We are all going to die. Accept this lesson from people who have gone before you: When you are sick or needy in any way, let those around you in. When you fail to do this, you increase the burden on the people closest to you who are going to have to live with the consequences of your

refusal, reluctance, or unwillingness to be cared
for the rest of their lives. If you want to take good
care of them let them take good care of you.

Before the procedure on the twenty-eighth, the doctors did a
CT scan to see how much the tumor had grown since June. After the
scan, I was moved back to the waiting room. After an hour's wait,
the nurse came and said, "That one didn't work out. We need to do
another one." I was requested to go through another scan.

While I waited for the results, I reflected on all the people who
had been there with me over the weekend celebrations. Would I ever
see them again? What a blessing they were to me. I felt so lifted up.
The people in the community of St. Nicholas had put on such a
wonderful reception. I was wondering how I could ever thank them
enough. All the people who said they were praying for me—how was
I going to pay all those people back?

And yet, here we go…what was this treatment going to be like?

Again, I sensed that awful taste of chemo in my mouth. I knew
this was the power of thought because it had been two months since
my last chemo treatment.

After another hour of waiting which seemed like two, I was
moved to the doctor's office. Dr. Witzig and Dr. Call came into the
room.

"Mark, we have no explanation…but your cancer has disappeared.

"We shared this with other doctors on staff here at the Mayo,
and we have no definitive answer as to why we cannot now detect
any tumors. We can detect a small spot where the tumor was, which
we are sure of, but we see no reason to do the procedure. This spot
may be scar tissue."

I didn't know what to say.

I was so ready to die. Now what?

I was also in awe and wonder. My heart welled up with emotion.

I have longer to live.

What do I do now? What do I say?

I have noticed a pattern in my life: God at times waits until the
last minute to answer prayers. This has been frustrating at times, but

I have learned that this time of pleading and waiting is never wasted. My spirit deepens and grows more rich and alive. While I wait for God to move, I am the one being moved and changed—always for the better.

I called Dad and Mom. They were very surprised and said, "That is great news!"

The papers took it from there. I, Mark Stang, this simple, shy farm boy, was in awe when I saw my name and picture in the headlines of the *Saint Cloud Times,* and then the *Minneapolis Tribune,* and then even a tabloid, the *National Examiner.* Someone even sent me a small article from *The New York Times.*

Before I knew it, radio and television stations asked to interview me. I remember flying out to Virginia to do a show on the Christian Broadcasting Network. Then EWTN. I began accepting invitations to give talks at conferences all around the United States. Again I felt so overwhelmed. Who is this shy farm boy now speaking in front of groups of thousands of people? I felt uncomfortable when people would ask me to share "my story" because so much was God's doing. All I had to do was let go and trust. It was never about me; it's all about God.

I am now a priest, and what a powerful call that is. My focus is on preaching, teaching, administering the sacraments, and serving the people. May God guide me and give me strength. All the glory to God!

Mission Continues

I took to heart that at three separate events, a bishop came up to me and said, "God has more work for you to do here before you die." I finished my priesthood study as a priest at St. John's University in Collegeville, Minnesota. I was assigned as a parochial vicar for two years at St. Andrew's in Elk River, Minnesota.

I then served as a pastor for twelve years at St. Mary of Mount Carmel in Long Prairie, Minnesota. Those wonderful parishioners took me under their wing and taught me how to be a priest. I am so grateful to them.

Then the bishop assigned me to serve a five-parish cluster at St. Mary's and St. Hedwig's in Holdingford, St. Columbkille in St. Wendel, Our Lady of Mount Carmel in Opole, and Immaculate Conception in St. Anna. While doing that assignment, I would occasionally take overnight coverage as a priest backup at the St. Cloud Hospital. I would be on call throughout the night to provide the sacraments in an emergency.

One night, I was called in to offer sacraments to a teenaged boy in the emergency room. He had been shot by his friend as they were playing with a gun in their living room. I provided the Last Rites for the boy before he died. The main chaplain was overwhelmed with being present to both the patient's family and his friend's family. I wanted to help out, so I spent time with the friend's family. After that evening was over, I felt I had not helped out at all. At times during the crisis event, I didn't have anything to say. There were long moments of just silence. I felt it was my job to have the answers for the grieving family. I had no answers. I felt so inadequate.

Days later, I really started questioning myself. I felt I had failed the family and that I could have done so much more. I was shocked when I received a beautiful, long letter from the family, thanking me for all I did for them. That's when I started reflecting that I really needed to learn more about hospital chaplaincy.

I asked my bishop if I could undertake a unit in clinical pastoral experience (CPE). This is a course that most seminarians take to practice ministering to patients in hospitals; however, my scheduled time to take this unit was when I was taking cancer treatment. He honored my request but informed me that serving five parishes and taking classes would be too much. I was assigned to the three-parish cluster of St. Francis De Sales in Belgrade, St. Donatus in Brooten, and SS. Peter and Paul in Elrosa.

In the spring of 2014, I completed the first unit of CPE. It was during my evaluation of this first unit with my supervisor that it became much more clear to me that my gifts could be used ministering to the sick at the hospital. Bret Reuter, the director of spiritual care in the St. Cloud Hospital, asked my bishop to assign me to serve as a full-time chaplain at the St. Cloud Hospital. When the bishop asked me, I told him, "I'll be there." There is freedom in obedience. I then completed the remaining three units of CPE at the St. Cloud Hospital and became a board-certified chaplain. This gave me a real sense of accomplishment. I felt more confident in myself yet still feel there is so much more to learn about myself and about life in general, especially end-of-life care.

Could it be that experience with cancer has helped my heart reach out to the suffering and those who have a terminal illness? I find myself in certain situations praying for life, whatever that life may be—whether it's life here longer on Earth or life with our Lord. My daily goal is not to have Mark Stang get in the way and do the speaking but to let Jesus Christ do the speaking through me. This is still a daily goal. Sometimes it works!

I do miss being a pastor out in a rural community. I miss inter-acting with the youth and attending their school events. I miss hav-ing a longer-term relationship with the people that I minister to. However, I also believe that this is where God has led me—to be a chaplain at a hospital. I feel so honored to be present to the people of God who are going through a crisis in their life or preparing to step out of this world and into the next.

Lord, the work You have for me to do on this earth has been extended. May all that You do through me and all the people that You touch give glory to Your name. Amen.

AFTERWORD

I am so grateful to my family as they walked this journey with me. We did have to make this walk again with my sister Jean. When she turned thirty-eight, she was ready to deliver her second child when she was diagnosed with brain cancer. She fought a courageous battle with the disease and treatments for nearly two years. We prayed so hard for a miracle like mine for Jean, but it didn't happen. She died leaving a husband and two beautiful children.

Jean had a habit of saying the date every day. She said this makes us grateful for the day. Sometimes we would do this when we went for an evening walk after the farm work was done. We would walk to the top of the hill on the driveway and watch the sunset. As the sun disappeared to where we could see only a little speck of it, she would say, "Last time we'll see the sun on August 19, 1980. Thank you, God." When she became a teacher, she would stop the class when the digital clock numbers lined up, as in 111 or 222, and say, "Happy minute!" My little sister taught me how to appreciate life and not take it for granted.

Her death caused me to question God—why did you give an extension of life on this earth for me but not for her and for the many, many, many other people who prayed for a miracle? This journey with Jean was yet another period of waiting for God to move and then accepting His will. This lesson and understanding of prayerful waiting, while frustrating, I believe has helped me to be a better chaplain. Sometimes there simply are no answers until we step into the next life.

I am also deeply grateful for all those who were so very patient and kind to me on this journey, especially my family, my spiritual directors Fr. Jerry Mahon, Fr. Robert Zylla, Fr. Anthony Manochio, and also Bishop Paul Dudley and Bishop Jerome Hanus, Fr. Paul Schmelzer, Fr. Roger Geditz, the religious in my family, and all those who prayed for me.

I thank God every morning for the gift of another day and extension of my life. I do this by putting my knees on the floor before I put my feet on the floor and saying a spontaneous surrender prayer that varies each day. I try to surrender my will to the will of God throughout the day.

Does it work? Well, my ego and my pride pretty much take over, and I have my life back "in control" by the time I'm done eating breakfast. It's a daily struggle to let go of the control and to trust in God. I try every day, but I certainly do not have this spirit of surrender perfected. It is my desire to just surrender each day and be an instrument of God. But you know, there are times when it works. I watch God do so much, and it's fun just to see it happen.

For example, one day at the hospital, I was walking down the hall when a nurse saw me and said, "Oh, wow—how did you know we needed you?" She invited me into a room where the patient was taking his last breaths. His family asked me if I would say a prayer. I was honored to provide the Apostolic Pardon and the Last Rites with the patient before he died. I often think I hope I can die this way. The family thanked me and said, "How did you know?" I encouraged them to just give glory to God. I'm just a simple farm boy—like anyone else. And an instrument for God—like everyone else.

As I told the *Morrison County Record* (December 21, 2003), "I really can't explain why things happened the way they happened, and why I am still alive and healthy today. However, I do realize that my life is really not mine anymore. It is so much now in God's hands, and I am very comfortable with it being there."

Even though I may have felt, when stepping out of my comfort zone, even to the point of darkness, that I am a fish out of the water, I know now that this was a time of great grace. Even though I didn't feel it, I *was* in God's life-giving water all along. By letting go and trusting God, I found myself in the merciful water of God's grace.

A prayer of surrender:

> *Lord, I thank You for another day of life. I surrender everything to You—all that I have, all my talents. Take me and lead me and guide me where You want me to go, whom You want me to meet, and what You want me to say. I surrender everything to You. Use me as You see fit to give You the glory. Send Your Holy Spirit to fill me and guide me. Amen.*

All of Fr. Mark's profits from sales of this book will be donated to help young men and women in the discernment of their vocation.

ABOUT THE AUTHOR

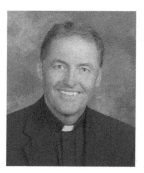

Rev. Mark Stang grew up on a family farm in St. Nicholas, Minnesota. A deeply spiritual man of few words who is at peace with life and death, he has a calming presence and an inner joy, knowing how short and how precious life is. He is challenged by weakness, but that is where he finds strength.

Currently, Father Mark is serving as a chaplain at St. Cloud Hospital in St. Cloud, Minnesota.

Carol Sanders is a retired English teacher and a former parishioner of Father Mark at St. Donatus Church in Brooten, Minnesota. She has published a few stories and articles. *Finding the Water* is her first full-length venture.

CPSIA information can be obtained
at www.ICGtesting.com
Printed in the USA
LVHW090253191219
641031LV00002B/568/P

9 781645 597032